The Technology of Farming

Producing Grains

Barbara A. Somervill

www.raintreepublishers.co.uk
Visit our website to find out more information about Raintree books.

To order:
☎ Phone 0845 6044371
🖷 Fax +44 (0) 1865 312263
🖳 Email myorders@raintreepublishers.co.uk

Customers from outside the UK please telephone +44 1865 312262

Raintree is an imprint of Capstone Global Library Limited, a company incorporated in England and Wales having its registered office at 7 Pilgrim Street, London, EC4V 6LB – Registered company number: 6695582

Edited by Abby Colich, Megan Cotugno, and Nancy Dickmann
Designed by Victoria Allen
Picture research by Elizabeth Alexander
Illustrations by Oxford Designers & Illustrators
Originated by Capstone Global Library Ltd
Printed and bound in China by China Translation and Printing Services Ltd

ISBN 978 1 406 24052 8
16 15 14 13 12
10 9 8 7 6 5 4 3 2 1

British Library Cataloguing in Publication Data

Somervill, Barbara A.
   Producing grains. -- (The technology of farming)
   1. Grain--Juvenile literature. 2. Grain trade--Juvenile literature. 3. Agricultural innovations--Juvenile literature.
   I. Title II. Series
   633.1-dc23
A full catalogue record for this book is available from the British Library.

Acknowledgements

We would like to thank the following for permission to reproduce photographs: Alamy: p. 6 (© Doug Peebles Photography); Corbis: pp. 7 (© Earl & Nazima Kowall), 12 (Frank Conlon); Getty Images: pp. 8 (Dagli Orti), 9 (Frederic J. Brown/ AFP), 11 (The Bridgeman Art Library), 35 (Bloomberg/ Patrick Fallon), 37 (AFP/ William West); Photolibrary: pp. 28, 33 (Still Pictures/Adrian Arbib), 34; © Sarah Montgomery/The Garden's Edge: p. 23; Shutterstock: pp. 5 (© Bernabea Amalia Mendez), 14 (© frog-traveller), 15 (© Fidel), 17 (© Heike Rau), 18 (© Robyn Mackenzie), 19 (© Frontpage), 20 (© Ildi Papp), 24 (© takayuki), 26 (© bogdan ionescu), 29 (© Kletr), 30 (© Mosista Pambudi), 31 (© Monkey Business Images), 42 (© Fishking), 43 (© Elena Elisseeva).

Cover photo of a combine harvesting wheat reproduced with permission from Shutterstock (© Kletr).

Every effort has been made to contact copyright holders of any material reproduced in this book. Any omissions will be rectified in subsequent printings if notice is given to the publisher.

Disclaimer

Contents

Some words appear in the text in bold, **like this**. You can find out what they mean by looking in the glossary.

Who eats grain?

The basic food of a person's diet is called a **staple**. Every culture has a staple food, and most staples are grains. The most common staples are rice, wheat, corn, and oats. We eat grains in bread and cereal. Grain can be a side dish, such as fried rice, or the main course, as with pasta. Grain is the main ingredient in pancakes, sandwiches, and pitta bread.

Rice is a staple food eaten three times a day in countries such as Japan. The Japanese eat *asagohan*, or "steamed morning rice", for breakfast. They may add soybean paste, seaweed, grilled fish, or rolled omelette. Japanese lunch boxes, called *bento*, contain rice, fish, vegetables, and fruit. In the evening, chicken or fish and vegetables are stir-fried and served with rice.

Wheat

One of the most popular grains worldwide is wheat. Wheat arrives on our tables in loaves of bread, rolls, pitta and naan bread, pasta and noodles. Even bread takes many forms. Bread can be thick, fluffy loaves of white bread, dense wholemeal bread, round flatbreads, or long, crusty baguettes.

Wheat can be the main ingredient in a meal, such as in pizza or lasagna. Wheat also can be part of a side dish, such as couscous. Bulgur wheat goes well with parsley and mint in *tabbouleh*, a Lebanese salad. Wheat is also used for making cakes, pies, tarts, and puddings.

Wholemeal bread provides energy, fibre, and protein.

A tradition of corn

Grinding corn by hand and making tortillas on a skillet is an ancient tradition in Central and South America. The basic ingredients for tortillas are simple: cornmeal and water. In the same way that rice is the staple of Chinese and Japanese diets, corn is the staple food in Mexico, Peru, Ecuador, and many Central American countries. Corn tortillas are served for breakfast, lunch, and dinner.

Corn has been eaten in Latin America for more than 9,500 years. Today it is eaten fresh as grilled corn on the cob. It is shaved off the cobs and cooked with courgettes or chillies. Corn is dried and ground into cornmeal for tortillas and cornbread.

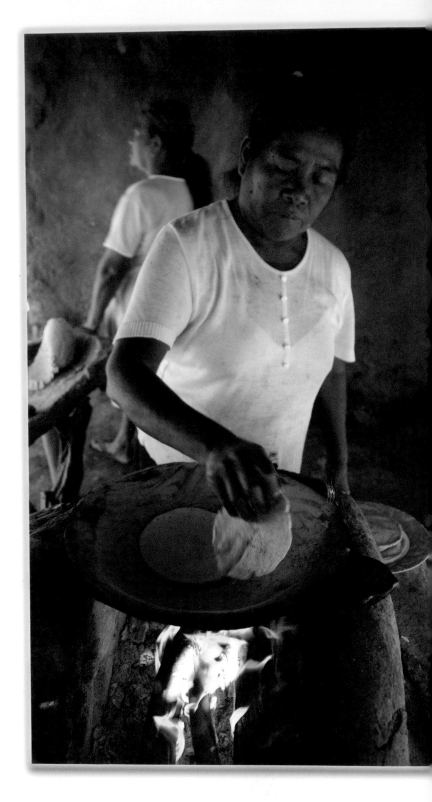

Many women still make tortillas by hand just as their grandmothers did.

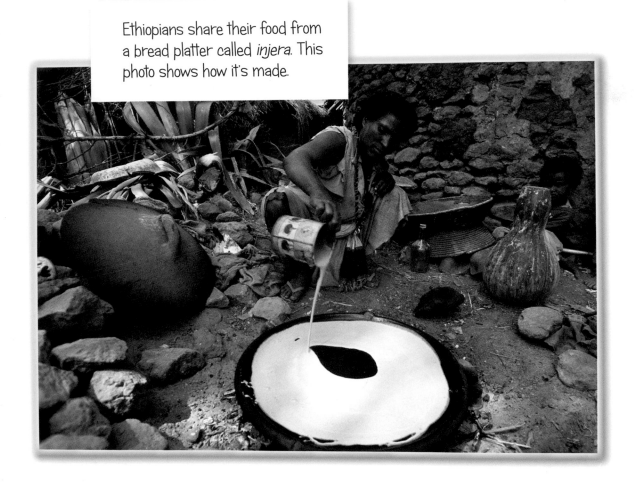

Ethiopians share their food from a bread platter called *injera*. This photo shows how it's made.

Breaking bread

Not all cultures cook with wheat, rice, or corn. Some people eat different staple grains, such as millet, kamut, oats, or teff. Teff is the main grain of Ethiopia, and is used to make *injera*. This is a round, flat bread about the size of a large pizza that is placed on a small tabletop. It serves as the bread, the plate, and the eating utensil of Ethiopian meals. Helpings of stew and vegetable dishes are spooned on to the *injera*. People tear off a small pieces of *injera* and use it to scoop up the food.

When did people start farming grain?

The first grains grew wild throughout the world. **Hunter-gatherer clans** collected nuts, berries, and grains. Clans followed large game animals. When clans had hunted until there were no more large game animals available, they had to find other food sources. They gathered seeds from wild grain, such as wheat or barley. People began to clear land and plant the seeds they collected. The seeds produced the first grain crops.

People began planting their own wheat as early as 10,000 BC in Syria, Jordan, and Turkey. People dried wheat berries and ground them to make flatbread. They began keeping farm animals and fed them leftover wheat straw. Some people wove the straw into sleeping mats, baskets, and **thatch** for roofs. By 5000 BC wheat farming had spread to Egypt's River Nile area. The Egyptians used wheat to make flour and alcohol.

The Egyptians followed a cycle of ploughing, planting, and **harvesting** wheat much as farmers do today.

Irrigation

The Chinese built the Dujjangyan **irrigation** system to water rice paddies. Water was lifted in buckets and dumped in the paddies. Although built 2,200 years ago, it is still in use.

Rice paddies need large amounts of standing water.

History of other grains

In the Americas, hunter-gatherers in present-day Mexico ate teosinte (an early type of corn) as early as 7500 BC. Corn became North America's first grain crop. By AD 1000 American Indians across the continent planted corn, beans, and squash in the same fields. Called the "Three Sisters", these crops fed native people throughout the year.

Rice farming began on the other side of the world. In roughly 2000 BC, southern China's wetlands yielded crops of wild rice. The planting and eating of rice spread westward along trade routes. Arabs brought rice planting to Spain in the AD 900s. By the 15th century, Italy, France, and Spain grew rice.

Growing grains became the foundation of **agriculture**. People saved some of the grain from the previous year for planting the following year. The type of grain grown depended on the **climate** and the soil. A new profession was born — the farmer.

Slow advances in technology

Over several thousand years, the tools used to grow grains slowly developed. Hand **ploughs** gave way to larger wooden ploughs pulled by horses or oxen. In Europe, farmers continued to use iron-tipped wooden ploughs until the 1700s, when Joseph Foljambe developed the first usable iron plough. Stronger iron ploughs allowed farmers to prepare more land for crops of wheat, rye, barley, and oats.

Planting seed was back-breaking work. People poked holes in the soil with small sticks, dropped in the seeds, and covered them with soil. In 1701, a British farmer named Jethro Tull (see box) developed a horse-drawn seed drill. The seed drill made planting more efficient.

Jethro Tull (1674–1741)

Jethro Tull farmed wheat in Berkshire. Tull saw the need for changes in grain farming. He promoted the use of horses for ploughing instead of oxen. Tull developed a mechanical seed drill and a horse-drawn hoe for clearing weeds. Many of Tull's farming ideas helped bring about a revolution in British agriculture.

Improving the harvest

To harvest the grain, farmers used **sickles** to cut it in much the same way that early Egyptians did. Eventually harvesters put curved blades, or sickles, on long sticks and created **scythes**. The act of cutting grain with scythes did not change until the mid-1800s. Harvesting grain required many people working many hours. In Europe entire communities worked together to bring in the harvest and then celebrated with a feast, singing, and dancing.

Rice plantations

One of the first grain crops to arrive in North America was rice. Although rice originated in Asia, it went to the American colonies from England. South Carolina landowners used ploughs and **dredges** to change swampland into rice **plantations**. By 1700, rice had become the main crop of South Carolina. The colony shipped rice to England, where the crop brought consistently high prices.

Threshers

Once the grain was cut, workers used **flails** to beat the grain. Flailing separated the grain from the husk. In 1784, Scottish engineer Andrew Meikle developed a mechanical **thresher**. Meikle's thresher was a major development for grain farming.

Farmers in the 1300s ploughed fields much like farmers did 1,000 years earlier.

McCormick's reaper

In 1834, the American inventor Cyrus Hall McCormick developed the **reaper**, which made harvesting easier. Farmers no longer needed a handful of men armed with scythes to cut their wheat crops. The reaper worked like a large, horse-drawn lawn mower.

A McCormick's reaper did the work of six men in less time.

Mechanizing grain farming

One thing that held back the production of grain was the amount of human work involved in ploughing, planting, and harvesting a crop. In 1830, it took about 250 to 300 work hours to produce less than 3 tonnes of wheat, which was the harvest from 2 hectares (5 acres).

By the mid-1800s farmers used steel ploughs to turn their fields. They used chemical **fertilizers** to increase their crops. Hand power changed to horse power as more farmers owned horses to help them with their work.

Petroleum power

In 1884, farmers used horse-drawn **combines** to harvest fields of wheat. By 1890, it needed only 40 to 50 working hours to produce 3 tonnes of wheat. The next advance in farming technology came in 1892, when John Froelich built the first petrol-driven tractor engine.

By 1965, it only took about 5 work hours to produce 3 tonnes of wheat. By this time, one farmer could grow enough grain, whether it was wheat, corn, barley, oats, or millet, to feed about 25 people for a year. Grain farming advanced far beyond hand ploughs and sickles.

John Froelich (1849–1933)

American inventor John Froelich was born in Iowa, USA. He attended the College of Iowa, where he became interested in building petrol-driven engines. In 1892, he produced a tractor with a 12-kilowatt (16-horsepower) engine. Froelich, a lifelong inventor, also developed a washing machine, a dishwasher and dryer, and a mechanical corn picker.

Mechanical picker

Mechanical reapers were no good for picking corn. In 1880, Patrick Lawler designed and built a mechanical corn picker, which poured out ears of husked corn. No one would buy them. Today, however, most corn farmers use mechanical corn pickers.

What exactly is grain?

Scientists define grain as the seed of a grass-like plant. This includes wheat, rice, corn, barley, and oats. These plants are types of grass, although they do not look like the grass of a lawn. There are hundreds of **species** of grass, and all of them flower and produce seeds.

Nutritionists would say that most seeds that are used whole as food or ground into flour are grain. **Amaranth**, **quinoa**, and buckwheat do not come from grass-like plants. They do produce seeds, and the seeds look like, taste like, and are used like grains. They are sold as grains in shops and can be ground into flour for breads and cakes just like wheat or corn.

A wheat plant is shown here with its kernels.

Wholegrains or processed grains

Wholegrains are the entire **kernel** or seed of grain. The outside, protective coating of the seed remains intact. The seeds can be eaten whole, such as with brown rice. They can be ground into flour, such as with wholemeal flour. Generally, wholegrain products have more protein, vitamins, and minerals than those made with **processed** grains.

Most of the **nutrients** in grain are found in the bran, which is the outer covering of grain seeds. Processed grains, such as white rice, remove the bran and lose much of their nutritional value. Brown rice is a wholegrain product. White rice is brown rice that has been milled to get rid of the outer bran coating.

Some flour, such as white wheat flour used for bread or cakes, is **enriched**. Enriching flour returns some of the nutrients lost from processing. Enriched white flour usually has thiamin, riboflavin, niacin, folic acid, iron, and calcium added to it.

Per cent of daily nutritional value per serving (174 grams)	Brown rice	White rice
Carbohydrate	15%	12%
Fibre	14%	7%
Protein	5%	4%
Iron	6%	1%
Calcium	2%	0%
Niacin	13%	3%
Vitamin B6	15%	2%
Manganese	107%	23%
Potassium	4%	0%

Brown rice provides more protein, vitamins, and minerals than white rice.

Definitely not a grass, buckwheat is actually related to rhubarb.

What are some other types of grain?

There are many grains that are not as popular as wheat, rice, or corn. Some of these grains, such as barley and oats, grow in many regions. Some grains grow mostly in their native region, such as **quinoa** from Peru and teff from Ethiopia.

Barley was a wild grain collected by **hunter-gatherers**. By 8000 BC barley was planted and grown as a crop in Mesopotamia, an area now known as Iraq and Syria. People ate barley as a breakfast cereal that was cooked like oatmeal. Today, barley mainly feeds animals and is used to make beer. While barley is easy to grow, it is hard to separate barley **groats** from the plant stalks.

Oats

Today, oats are extremely popular in many places around the world. Like most other grains, oats were the seeds of wild grasses. They were often found as weeds in early Egyptian wheatfields. The earliest evidence of oat grains were found in Egypt and date back to about 2000 BC. Evidence of farmed oats has also been found in caves in Switzerland.

People eat oats in porridge, biscuits, flapjacks, and granola bars. Oats are highly nutritious. Eating oats is known to reduce **cholesterol** in human blood. The grain can help control blood pressure and reduce the chance of getting cancer. When added to bathwater, oats can help soothe itchy chicken pox, **eczema**, and sunburn. Oats are also used as cattle and horse feed.

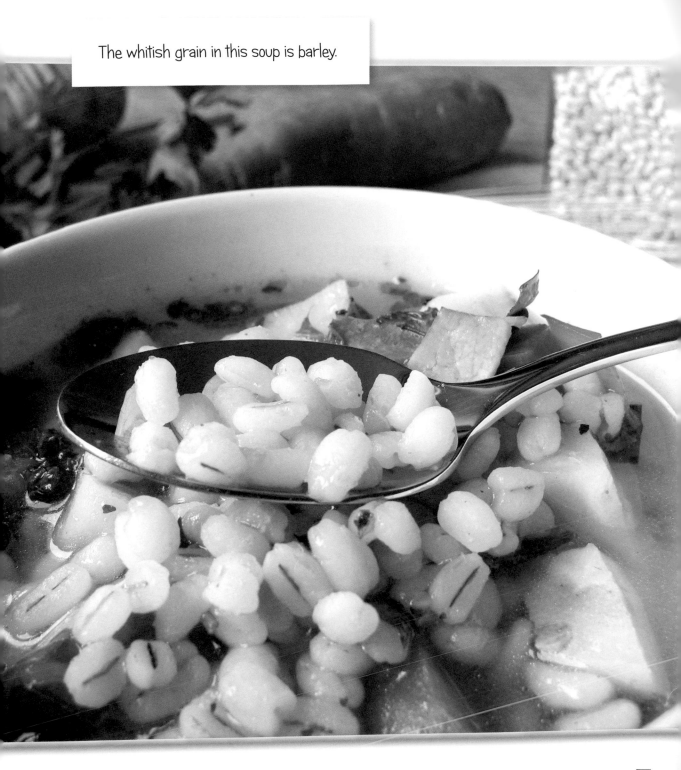

The whitish grain in this soup is barley.

Rye

Long regarded as a weed growing among wheat crops, rye eventually became a farmed grain in cold, northern **climates**. Rye also grows well in high, dry desert areas. It is a traditional grain used for making bread and alcohol in Northern Europe, Russia, the United States, and Canada.

Rye is unusual among grains for its high fibre content. Fibre is important for a healthy digestive system. With most grains, the human body converts the grain starches to sugars for energy. Rye does not produce as much blood sugar as other grains, such as wheat or corn. This makes rye especially healthy for **diabetics**, who must limit their sugar intake.

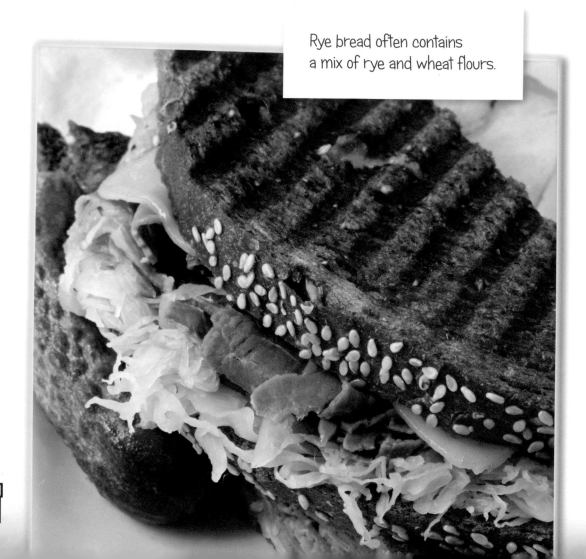

Rye bread often contains a mix of rye and wheat flours.

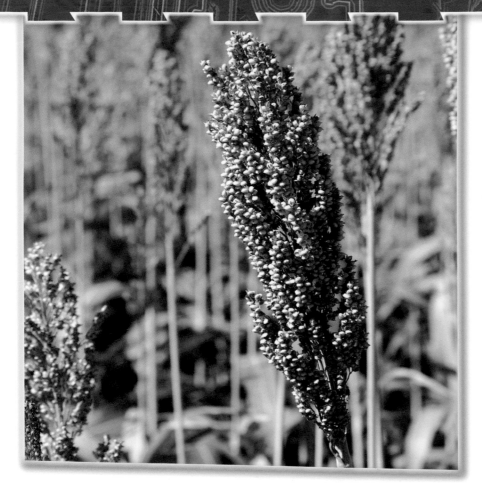

Millet makes good cattle feed. which is important in places where there is no grass for grazing.

Millet

For thousands of years, millet grew wild in Africa and Asia. The grass grows to about 1.5 to 3 metres (5 to 10 feet) tall and looks like thin corn stalks. Millet needs little rain and can grow where wheat and barley cannot. This makes it an ideal crop for regions with poor soil, little rainfall, and high temperatures.

Scientists believe that hunter-gatherers ate wild millet more than 10,000 years ago. As with wheat, people began collecting the seeds first, and they did not begin to plant millet as a farm crop until about 4500 BC in China. In Sudan, millet was first farmed about 4000 BC. The grain is used to make beer or eaten as a hot breakfast cereal. Millet can also be added to soups, stews, or vegetable dishes. It provides protein, vitamin B, calcium, iron, and potassium.

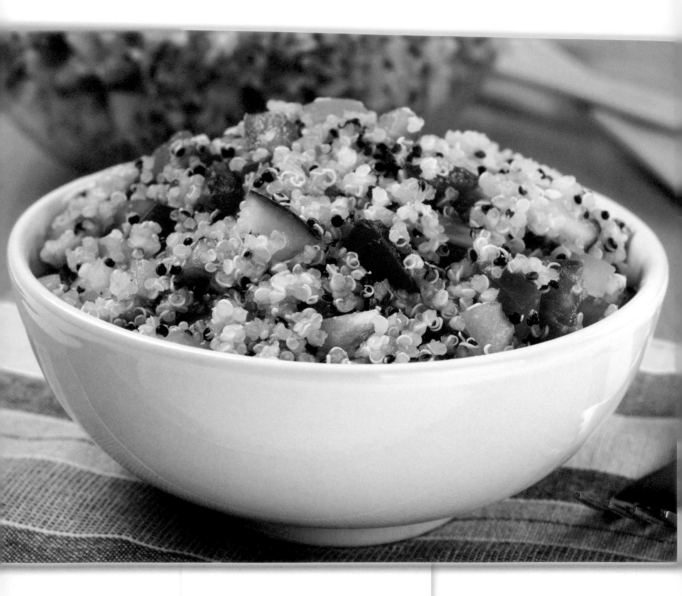

Quinoa comes in many colours,
including white (shown here),
purple, red, and black.

Buckwheat

Buckwheat flour is popular in many countries around the world. It is most commonly used in American pancakes, Japanese soba noodles, and a Russian porridge called *kasha*. Buckwheat seeds, called groats, provide a rich, nutty flavour to food.

Buckwheat can flourish in rocky regions where it is hard to grow wheat or corn. It is not a true grass or a grain, but the groats are so "grain-like" that buckwheat is generally considered a type of grain. Buckwheat can be eaten fresh and raw, or dried and ground into flour. It can thicken soups or gravies or be baked into flatbread. Pillows and furniture filled with buckwheat hulls are popular for people who are **allergic** to feathers.

Quinoa

Quinoa is pronounced *keen-wah*. The Incas raised quinoa high in the Andes Mountains of South America. The seeds have been collected and **processed** since about AD 1200. Like buckwheat, quinoa is not technically a grass or a grain. It is generally considered to be a grain because it can be eaten as seeds or as flour. Quinoa seeds are small and look very like sesame seeds. They come in brown, red, purple, and black. Most quinoa still comes from the Andes, but the plants also grow well in the Rocky Mountains of North America.

Quinoa can be added to soups, pastries, cakes, and salads. The ground flour is often added to breakfast cereal flakes. Quinoa provides protein, magnesium, and fibre in diets. Because it contains no **gluten**, quinoa is good for people on gluten-free diets.

Why are ancient grains making a comeback?

Ancient grains sound like something taken from Egyptian tombs, but they are eaten every day. Most ancient grains are sold in health-food shops and some supermarkets. The grains can also be found in some modern, wholegrain breads. Ancient grains include spelt, **amaranth**, **quinoa**, teff, **farro**, and kamut.

What makes a grain ancient as opposed to modern? Ancient grains have not changed for thousands of years. Compare amaranth to corn. Amaranth grown today grows, looks, and tastes like amaranth grown 2,000 years ago. Today's corn has been bred to produce neat, tidy rows of yellow or white **kernels**. It looks nothing like the corn the Aztecs grew 1,000 years ago. The corn that the Aztecs ate had blue, purple, red, and yellow kernels. When the kernels were dried and ground, Aztec cornmeal was a shade of dark blue.

High food value

Ancient grains are prized for the food value they provide. Most deliver high amounts of protein and fibre. For people with **gluten** allergies, quinoa, amaranth, and spelt have low gluten content. Yet these grains contain all the vitamins and minerals needed for good nutrition. Ancient grains have become part of a health-food revolution.

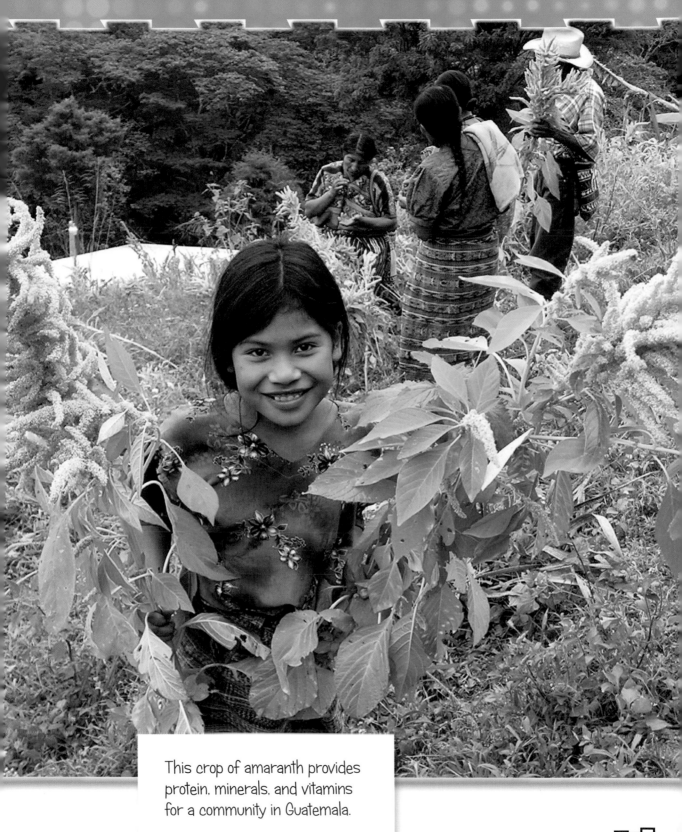

This crop of amaranth provides
protein, minerals, and vitamins
for a community in Guatemala.

How do we use grain?

It is obvious that grain is used for food. We feed cattle, dairy cows, poultry, and other livestock on grain, so, indirectly, our meat, poultry, and dairy products also come from grain. Wheat or corn is eaten, in one form or another, at nearly every meal in developed countries. For 60 per cent of the world, rice appears on the table daily. What most people do not know is that there are hundreds of uses for grain that do not include food. One advantage of using grains to make nonfood products, such as plastics or oils, is that grains are **renewable**. Farmers can grow more grain.

This lovely red parasol is made from rice paper.

People who have plenty of rice have found clever ways to use this grain. Rice makes excellent animal food and is often put in dog and cat food. Rice straw — the dried stalks — make a good base for growing mushrooms. The straw also makes strong paper, which can be used in printing and as a food. The starchy nature of rice lends itself to being the base of rice glue, which is essential for Japanese paper crafts.

Working with wheat

Wheat consists of the straw-like stalks and berries, or grain. All parts of wheat plants are used in making a wide variety of products. Because wheat is a high-protein grain, it makes good feed for farmed fish and for turkeys. The grain absorbs water and is often an ingredient in cat litter. Wheat is also used to make biodegradable plastics, such as coffee cups and plastic forks and spoons.

One common characteristic of wheat is that it contains **gluten**. Some people are **allergic** to gluten, so they must watch what they eat. They also need to watch out for which cosmetics they use. Wheat or wheat gluten is found in face creams, shampoos and conditioners, lipstick, foundation make-up, and powder.

The most useful grain: corn

A full list of all the uses for corn would take pages. Corn, corn oil, cornstarch, and corn syrup are used to make hundreds of food products, from tortilla wraps to gravy granules to lemonade. There is even corn in chewing gum. Scientists use corn in many surprising ways, including in **ethanol**, which is a common ingredient in car fuel.

Crayons actually contain corn!

In an average day, people come into contact with dozens of corn products without even knowing it. Shaving cream and disposable nappies contain corn products. The crayons children use to colour with and the latex paint on kitchen walls also have corn in them. Corn is in wallpaper and the glue that sticks wallpaper to the walls. It is also in **antibiotics**, such as penicillin, and aspirin.

Like wheat, corn is used in many types of personal products. Many face creams, shampoos and conditioners, and deodorants use a chemical that comes from corn oil. Corn-based chemicals are also found in face powder, blusher, lipstick, and mascara.

Corn is also used in some unusual products. Few people would expect that corn is used in manufacturing spark plugs or batteries. Corn is part of the process that makes fireworks. Even the insulation that keeps homes warm depends in part on corn.

James Caleb Jackson (1811–1895)

James Caleb Jackson invented the first dry, wholegrain breakfast cereal. Jackson worked at a healthcare centre in New York State, USA. He believed that diet was an important part of good health. In 1863 he developed Granula, a breakfast cereal made from wholemeal flour called Graham flour.

How does grain get from the field to the market?

Grain ripens in the field, and then it is harvest time. In many countries, farmers drive huge **combines** in neat rows through the crops. Combines **harvest** grain crops quickly, leaving an empty field behind.

In some countries, grain is still harvested by hand. Workers cut the grain with **scythes** or use **reapers** drawn by horses, mules, or oxen. Other workers **thresh** the grain. Workers collect the stalks, which may be used to feed cattle or to stuff bedding. The grain must also be cleaned. This process, called **winnowing**, separates the usable grain from the husks, called **chaff**. Bringing in the harvest is hard, backbreaking work.

Heavy millet grain falls to the ground. while lighter husks blow away.

A combine cuts and threshes grain in one quick process.

Storing grain

On a modern farm, grain that is kept for cattle feed is stored in silos. Grain being sent to market is loaded on to lorries or goods trains and transported. The grain may be put into sacks, or it may be shipped in bulk. With bulk shipping, loose grain fills a large container. The container protects the grain from rain or wind.

Combine harvester

Combine harvesters (or simply "combines") take much of the work out of harvesting grain crops. The machines do three jobs at one time. They reap the harvest. They thresh the grain, separating grain from husks. And they clean the crop. Combines are used to harvest wheat, oats, and rye.

At the mill

Grain destined as food for people is packaged for sale in markets. The grain may need to be washed to get rid of dirt, plant remains, or insects. Some grain is sold as whole grain, and some is sold as flour.

Breakfast cereal manufacturers, commercial bakeries, and pet food companies may buy whole grains by the lorry-load. These companies may grind the grain themselves. The grain may also go to a mill to be **processed**. The mill packages flour or processed grains for sale in supermarkets and for use by manufacturers.

This rice mill removes the bran from brown rice, producing white rice.

More than just bread

Wheat and rye flour are commonly found in bread. Cornmeal is also used in baking, as are oats, sorghum, and buckwheat. Pasta, noodles, rice products, baked desserts, and breakfast cereals line the aisles of supermarkets. They are all obvious grain products.

Some less obvious grain products include soft drinks, pet food, and snack foods. Corn syrup is an ingredient in confectionary and ketchup. Oats are one of the main ingredients in granola bars. Grain products provide ingredients used to make some yoghurts and dessert toppings. Corn syrup appears in pickles, jams, sauces, and salad dressings. In fact, a look at the ingredients of many grocery items shows a surprising number of grain products in common foods.

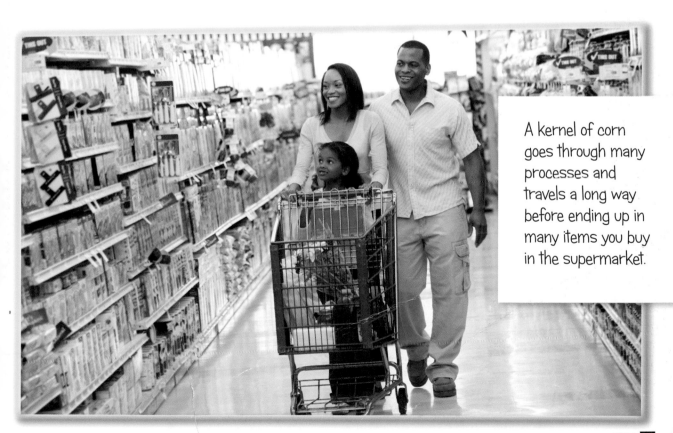

A kernel of corn goes through many processes and travels a long way before ending up in many items you buy in the supermarket.

Can science produce more grain?

Biotechnology is using living organisms to make or manufacture something people want to use. It includes the study of ways to make plants or animals grow bigger, produce more crops, or resist disease. In nature, the stronger, hardier plants thrive. Some people worry about new **species** developed by scientists, particularly when it involves **genetic engineering**. But many scientists argue that biotechnology is just working with nature's process of natural selection in laboratories.

For many years, developing countries have been unable to feed their people. Poor soil, **drought**, insects, and plant diseases resulted in poor crops. The **green revolution** uses science to develop grain species that survive in poor conditions. Scientists find ways to help developing nations feed themselves by making grains that succeed where other crops fail. The green revolution has produced wheat that thrives in Mexican deserts and high Indian plains. It has produced high-yield rice and larger ears of corn.

Norman Borlaug (1914–2009)

Norman Borlaug, a plant scientist from Iowa, USA, developed a form of short-stalk, high-yield wheat. His efforts won him the Nobel Peace Prize in 1970 for engineering wheat that would help feed the world. Borlaug is considered the founder of the green revolution. He also founded the World Food Prize in 1986 to recognize scientists that contribute to the world food supply.

Farming in labs

It might seem that wheat is wheat and rice is rice. That is not so. Different species of wheat, for example, grow better in one **climate** than another. They yield more wheatberries and have different food values. Hard red spring wheat has more protein than soft red winter wheat. Durum wheat contains more niacin than hard white wheat. In all, there are several hundred varieties of wheat seeds, and nearly all wheat seeds are **hybrids**.

When developing a hybrid, scientists try to grow a new generation of plants with the best characteristics from two other plants. For example, one type of wheat grows well in dry areas. Another type resists plant diseases. Scientists try to produce a new wheat variety that has both of these characteristics. This process is called **selective breeding**.

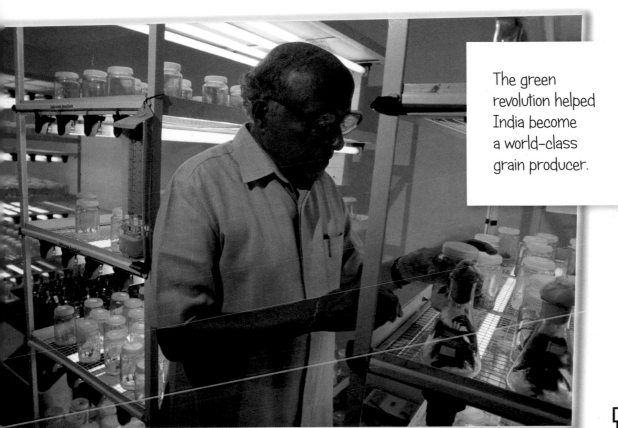

The green revolution helped India become a world-class grain producer.

Genetically engineered grain

We have been eating **genetically modified** (GM) grains for years. Nearly all wheat, rice, and corn are hybrids of grains grown hundreds of years ago. Aztec corn featured uneven yellow, blue, and purple **kernels**. The tidy, pale yellow corn we eat today is a hybrid of Aztec corn.

Here are three ways scientists have developed "better" rice. The amount of rice grown in the world is not enough to feed everyone who would normally eat rice. Scientists developed high-yield rice that increased rice crops by 15 to 20 per cent. A newly developed "super rice" delivers three times the crop of normal rice. Golden rice, another product of lab science, has more vitamin A than normal rice. In diets that lack vitamin A, golden rice fills that gap.

This type of hybrid rice produces 30 per cent more rice per plant than normal rice plants.

Ethanol is fuel made from corn or other plant matter.

Grain into fuel

Another area in which biotechnology has made great changes is the production of **ethanol**. Used since the 1820s, ethanol was the fuel Henry Ford used to power his first Ford motor car. The value of biofuel is that it may take the place of petroleum products. Petroleum is not a **renewable** resource, but the grains used to produce biofuel can be grown and **processed** in many places. Ethanol is a corn-based product. Biodiesel may be made from a variety of different seed oils.

Who buys and sells grain?

Throughout the world the success of grain depends on several factors. Grain needs the Sun, good soil, and water. Too much water or **drought** conditions destroy crops. Natural disasters such as hurricanes, floods, insects, and plant diseases destroy grain crops. The loss of a crop affects human diets by reducing the amount of grain we eat. Loss of grain crops also affects our protein sources. Beef cattle, poultry, farmed fish, pigs, and sheep eat grains. The loss of grains will reduce the amount of meat, chicken, or fish available and increase the cost of that food.

Case study: Australia's drought

Over the past decade, Australia's major grain-producing region has suffered drought. Australian rice crops are down to 2 per cent of what they were 10 years ago. Once, Australia sold extra rice. Today, the country needs to import rice. Wheat crops are nearly as bad. Australia normally grows 15 per cent of the world's wheat. When wheat crops fail, farmers lose their farms and the country's economy suffers.

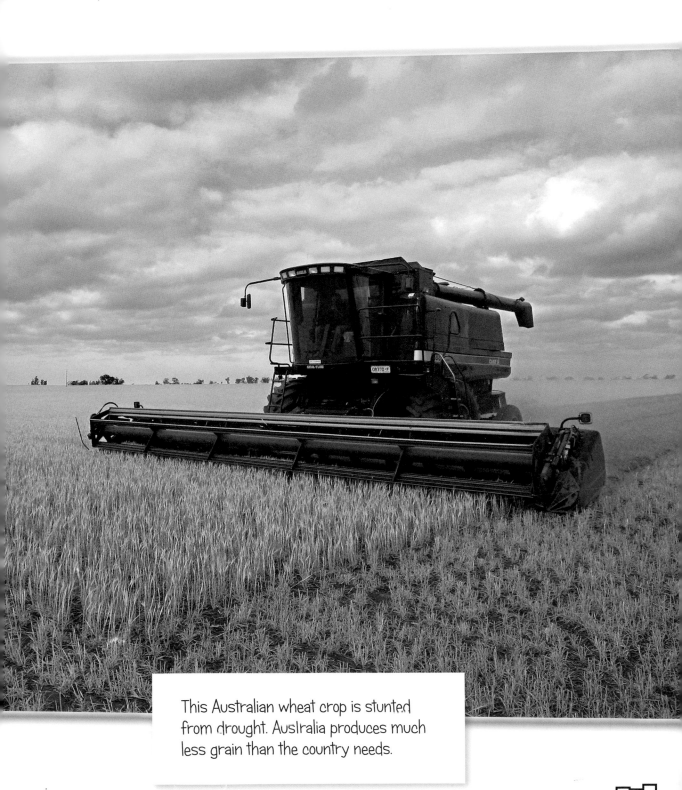

This Australian wheat crop is stunted from drought. Australia produces much less grain than the country needs.

Changing wheat production

Wheat production has changed. India and China now grow more wheat than the United States or Russia. The developing world's share of wheat production is about 60 per cent of the total world crop. Major wheat users in Asia include China, India, Iran, Pakistan, and Turkey.

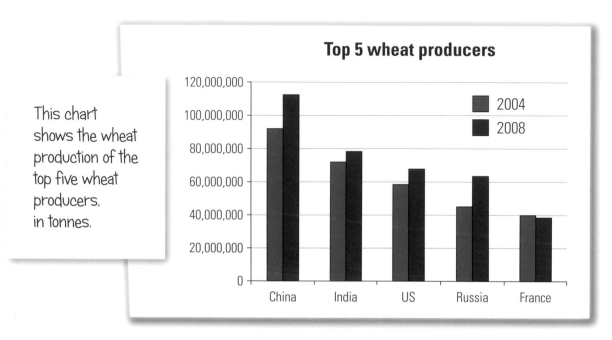

This chart shows the wheat production of the top five wheat producers, in tonnes.

Top 5 wheat producers

Rice production

According to the United Nations Food and Agriculture Organization (FAO), 93.3 per cent of the world's rice production comes from seven countries. China and India grow the most rice. They also eat most of the rice they grow. Japan, a major rice consumer, is facing a serious rice shortage. Japan can no longer grow enough rice to feed its people. In 2011, Japan suffered an earthquake and tsunami. The tsunami deposited salt in the soil of the Tohoku region of northern Japan. Tohoku grows 26 per cent of Japan's rice. In recent years, Japan has imported 600,000 tonnes (660,000 tons) of rice per year. If the rice fields of Tohoku fail, Japan will need to import even more rice.

Other grains

The European Union and Russia are the world's largest producers of barley, rye, and oats. Russia, Canada, and Ukraine use the most barley. Rye is one of the few grains that can be used in making yeast bread. Northern European countries, such as Belarus, Poland, and Germany, use large amounts of rye, but Russia is the largest consumer of this grain. Oats are commonly used to feed cattle and horses or as hot breakfast cereal. Russia, the United States, and Canada consume the most oats.

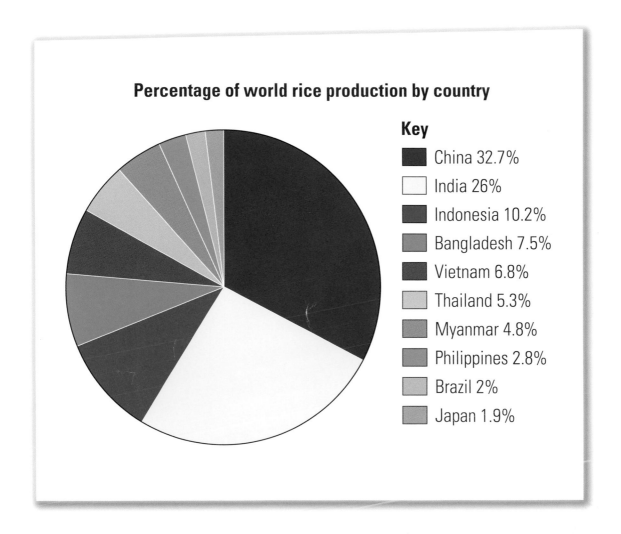

Percentage of world rice production by country

Key

- China 32.7%
- India 26%
- Indonesia 10.2%
- Bangladesh 7.5%
- Vietnam 6.8%
- Thailand 5.3%
- Myanmar 4.8%
- Philippines 2.8%
- Brazil 2%
- Japan 1.9%

Can grains end world hunger?

Despite the ability of some nations to produce large quantities of grain, the world does not grow enough grain to feed everyone. **Drought**, war, and disease leave millions of people unfed or underfed. Grains are important in the fight against hunger. They provide nutrition and energy and are fairly inexpensive. A bowl of brown rice costs only pennies compared to the price of chicken or beef.

Relief agencies such as the United Nations World Food Programme try to feed those without enough food in several ways. They ship grain to regions where hungry people live. It is not easy to ensure the grain reaches those who need it. Agencies work with farmers to help the hungry feed themselves. They help dig wells and provide quality seed for growing grains.

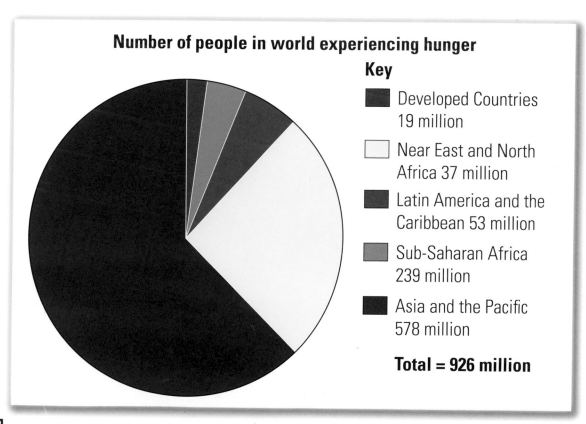

Number of people in world experiencing hunger

Key
- Developed Countries 19 million
- Near East and North Africa 37 million
- Latin America and the Caribbean 53 million
- Sub-Saharan Africa 239 million
- Asia and the Pacific 578 million

Total = 926 million

In 2011, more than half of people without enough food in the world lived in Asia.

People causing hunger

While it is easy to blame nature for crop failure, humans also cause hunger. War destroys crops, displaces people, and leaves many people with no way to feed themselves. Greed also gets its share of blame. Too often grain sent to relieve hunger is stolen and sold by people in power.

The cycle of hunger

Turning barren land into grain crops is not quick or easy. In many places, farmers do not have modern technology to plough, seed, or water their fields. They **harvest** and process grain by hand. Poor seed planted in worn-out soil produces low-yield crops. The solution to this problem is educating farmers on better ways of growing grain. That step includes providing tractors and harvesters. It also depends on seed that will grow drought-resistant, high-yield grain.

Gebisa Ejeta (born 1950)

One of Africa's biggest problems is growing grain in drought-ridden areas. Ethiopian Gebisa Ejeta bred a **hybrid** type of sorghum that grows with very little water. Sorghum is usually eaten as porridge or fed to livestock. Ejeta won the World Food Prize in 2009 for his work in developing hardy types of sorghum to feed the hungry in Ethiopia and Sudan.

Robotic rice planter

Robotic rice planters can plant a rice paddy in far less time and more efficiently than humans. Cutting down on human labour and planting more productive types of rice will increase rice crops. Asian people depend on rice as a **staple** in their diets. Rice planters can help feed Asia's hungry.

A robotic rice planter takes the labour out of planting rice in Japan.

This wheat is ready for harvest.

The solution

The solution to hunger is to teach **sustainable** grain farming. Sustainable grain farming means taking advantage of every plot of usable soil. It means conserving soil and water. Sustainable farming requires proper grain storage that reduces grain loss. In recent years, nearly 40 per cent of grain harvested in developing countries rotted in poor storage facilities. Distributing grain is an issue that needs improvement. For example, in 2010 45,000 tonnes (50,000 tons) of wheat in India sat in railroad cars and spoiled. India has too many hungry people to have this kind of waste.

High-yield, productive grain seed can produce more grain, but seed is only one aspect of a very large problem. There is no quick solution to world hunger. This is a complex issue that includes farming technology, soil quality, **irrigation**, better seed quality, and **fertilizer**. Countries that produce large quantities of grain need to help those that struggle, farm by farm and crop by crop.

Glossary

agriculture job of farming or growing crops

allergic having a strong negative reaction to a substance

amaranth flowering plant grown for food

antibiotics substances that kill bacteria

biotechnology use of living things to produce products or improve the environment

chaff grain husks

cholesterol group of solid fats found in animal blood

clan group of related people

climate general weather conditions of an area

combine machine that reaps, threshes, and cleans grain

diabetic person whose body has difficulty using sugars and starches

dredge machine used for moving earth

drought long period without sufficient rainfall

eczema skin problem that causes red, itchy, or scaly skin

enrich treat with added protein, vitamins, or minerals

ethanol fuel made from plant fibres

farro food made with wholewheat grains

fertilizer chemical substance that helps plants grow

flail tool used to separate grain from its husks by beating the grain

genetic engineering science of changing the genetic make-up of a living thing

genetically modified substances that have been changed at their most basic level

gluten gluey substance found in wheat or rye flour

green revolution scientific effort to help developing countries grow better crops

groats hulled kernels of grain

harvest collect a crop

hunter-gatherer early human who lived by hunting and collecting food but had no fixed home base

hybrid offspring of plants produced by crossbreeding two species of the same plant

irrigation system of watering plants

kernel soft, edible part of grain

nutrient substance that sustains life, health, or growth, such as vitamins and minerals

nutritionist person trained in determining foods that support life, health, or growth

plantation large farm dedicated to one main crop

plough tool used to break up soil

processed treated or prepared for use

quinoa ancient grain-like food of the Incas

reaper mechanical grain cutting machine

renewable able to be reproduced

scythe long-handled cutting tool

selective breeding process of developing new types of plants with the best characteristics of parent plants

sickle short-handled, curved blade

species class of individuals having common characteristics or traits

staple basic food of a person's diet

sustainable able to last a long time

thatch plant material used to cover a roof

thresh to separate grain from chaff

thresher machine that separates grain from chaff

winnowing freeing grain from its husks

Find out more

Books

Earth-Friendly Food (How to be Earth Friendly), Gillian Gosman
(Powerkids Press, 2011)

Farming Vegetables and Grains (Ethics of Food), Michael Burgan (Raintree, 2011)

Food and Farming (Changes in...), Steve Parker (QED Publishing, 2009)

Grains (Food Groups), Lola Schaefer (Heinemann Library, 2008)

John Deere (History Maker Bios), Jane Sutcliffe (Lerner, 2007)

Sustainable Farming (How Can We Save Our World?), Carol Ballard
(Franklin Watts, 2009)

The Story Behind Bread (True Stories), Elizabeth Raum (Heinemann Library, 2010)

Websites

Alternative Grains
You can find out more at this website about alternative grains such
as amaranth, kamut, quinoa, millet, spelt, and wild rice.

www.alive.com/2102a5a2.php?subject_bread_cramb=491

Kids Corner - Grains, they're essential!
Find out still more about the history of grain farming and bread-making.

http://www.grainsessential.ca/english/kids/history_1.html

History of wheat
This website discusses the history of wheat. As farming improved, so
did the grain. The amount of grain harvested also increased. Find out
how wheat became the plant that changed the world!

www.allaboutwheat.info/history.html

UK Centre for Living Foods

Learn more about grains at this website of the United Kingdom Centre for Living Foods. Grains have been cultivated for thousands of years for their nutrient value. Our ancestors collected grains, ground them by hand, and thrived on their nutrition.

www.livingfoods.co.uk/pages/articles/grains.php

Places to Visit

Agricultural shows

A great way to see farm animals and all the latest farm machinery is to visit an agricultural show. These shows often have livestock competitions and other agricultural events as well. Check on the internet to find a show near you that welcomes visitors.

The Agricultural Museum at Brook

The Street
Brook, Ashford, Kent

www.agriculturalmuseumbrook.org.uk

Shugborough Hall, Staffordshire

Step back in time and visit a working Georgian farm at Shugborough Hall in Staffordshire. See how the millwheel produces fine, wholemeal flour, and watch dairymaids demonstrate 19th century methods of making butter and cheese.

www.shugborough.org.uk/home-10

Index